The

Book

On

Music

Lessons

Publisher: RAMAtic Press

Cover Design: Brannon Hungness

Production and Composition: RAMAtic Productions

ISBN: 978-0-692-27385-2

www.RochesterMusicLessons.com

www.VirtualAcademyofMusic.com

Photos provided by
Rochester Academy of Music & Arts

Special thanks to Yunjin Audrey Kim

The Book on Music Lessons

A fun and easy-to-read guide about finding the right music lessons for you or a loved one

By
Brannon Hungness

Edited by Brigid Harrigan

RAMAtic Press

About the Author

Brannon Hungness is a professional musician who has performed throughout the US, Europe, and Canada, sharing the stage with Elvis Costello, Philip Glass, Iggy Pop, and many others. He has recorded with musicians from the Paul McCartney Band, Pink Floyd, Peter Gabriel Band, The Fixx, and the list goes on and on.

Mr. Hungness is known as Rochester NY's most sought-after music education authority. He founded the Rochester Academy of Music & Arts in 2007, realizing a life-long dream to create an institute famous for its dazzling creativity and attention to the interests and goals of each individual student.

Throughout the years, Brannon Hungness and the Rochester Academy of Music & Arts have won many awards, both locally and nationally.

In 2016, *The Book on Music Lessons* became a #1 bestseller on Amazon.

Mr. Hungness has been seen on BBC, NBC & MTV2.

Working with some of the best musicians in the world!
(From left: Joe Locke, Brannon Hungness, Jerry Marotta, Tony Levin, with sound
engineer Calvin May) Photo by Eric Taylor

Brannon Hungness after winning a national award for
Music Academy Excellence and Business Growth.

Introduction

I believe that everyone loves music.

Most people have at least a general interest and a few favorite songs.

Some people have a favorite band or artist, and make it their mission collect every recording they can get their hands on.

Other people really connect with a certain style of music, which influences how they dress and decorate their living spaces.

Many social groups have formed based on common tastes in music.

Often, just listening to a song can make a bad day seem a little brighter. Even if they don't consciously realize it, music plays an important part in most people's lives. Sometimes, people even take the next step and become musicians themselves.

Getting a guitar for Christmas at the age of 5 started my journey to becoming a musician. After playing around with the instrument for a few years, my parents signed me up for lessons when I was 7.

When I was 14, I had my first public performance and subsequently began teaching out of my parents' house. This was exciting, as the money I made could be used to buy more musical gear!

I was a decent teacher when I started, but I wasn't the best. My students liked me well enough, and most of them learned a good deal from me. However, the only way I knew how to teach was by showing them what my teachers had shown me.

But all that was about to change. You see, I didn't know it then, but my life was going to take me on a quest to discover the secrets of being a *SUPER FANTASTIC AMAZING MUSIC TEACHER*!

Throughout high school I taught at a nearby music store. Actually, I started teaching there because the owner heard me trying out a guitar he had for sale. When he heard the sounds I was making with his merchandise, he immediately rushed over and asked if I could give **him** lessons!

So I started teaching him and other students at his store. I was the local hotshot, but looking back, not such a hot teacher. Don't get me wrong! I was better than the other teachers around me, but I still had so much to learn.

Throughout college and into early adulthood, I continued giving private guitar lessons. Eventually, I also started teaching piano, bass, voice, drums, saxophone, ukulele, mandolin, and few other instruments.

After college, my career took off as a performing and recording artist. I spent the better part of 4 years on the road and in the studio. That experience could fill a whole other book, so I won't delve into it here!

Although I continued to live in that world, I was also excited to get back into teaching. This time, my life experiences had opened my eyes and given me a whole new mindset. I was ready to give my students the best of me.

It was during this period that I really began concentrating on becoming a great teacher. The "SUPER FANTASTIC AMAZING MUSIC TEACHER" I mentioned earlier!

That was 1997. For the next 10 years, I built my resume by teaching at some of the most well-known music stores and music schools in the Rochester New York area. I also taught from my home and traveled to the homes of various students. (Later in this book, I will tell you why it's best to take lessons at a school.)

In 2007, I opened my own music academy, the Hungness School of Music, which I later renamed **Rochester Academy of Music & Arts.**

At first, it was just me. I taught all the instruments and ran every aspect of the business myself.

The pressure was on! I had to pay the rent. I had to pay for marketing and promotion. Other expenses were, at times, **completely unexpected, and completely overwhelming!**

During the 10 years prior to opening my business, I worked very hard on honing my teaching chops.

Through trial and error, I reached the point where I felt I could start my own school and make it.

And you know what? I did it!

Because I had spent so much time focused on enhancing my teaching skills, I was able to keep students engaged and wanting more! **We were having fun!**

As the academy grew, I got more teachers involved. We've been growing every year since.

I was a good teacher before I started my school, but I became 10x better on my own. Surviving under incredible stress. Pushing myself. And, most importantly, listening to my students and learning from them how I could become better.

So, with this book, you now have a quick start guide to music lessons. *The Book on Music Lessons* has now become a #1 bestseller and has helped students all across the country and I'm very thankful for its success.

It's true that the information about music lessons that you will find in this book comes from my years of teaching experience. But it also results from my dedication to learning. And from laying it all on the line, in the belief that I could create the best music school in the world.

When focusing on educating others, we sometimes forget that the most important trait that good teachers share is their ability and willingness to learn. So thank you to all the students I not only taught, but from whom I also learned so much from.

And thanks to you, dear reader. I hope you will learn a lot as well. Learning is a life-changing gift!

All the best,

Brannon Hungness

Revised April 4th, 2017

Rochester New York

The Book on Music Lessons

This book is dedicated to future musicians everywhere. We're waiting to *hear you*!

Chapter 1

10 Benefits of learning to play a musical instrument

Wow! Did you know that playing a musical instrument can change the structure of your brain?

This may sound like something out of a sci-fi movie, but it is actually a medically proven phenomenon! And even better, these particular brain changes offer many positive benefits.

So let's choose 10 benefits and look at them in detail. There are many more, but these are some of the most important.

1. Our thought processes are improved.

Musically trained people typically outperform non-musically trained people on cognitive tasks.

They perform better on tests of word recall, nonverbal memory, and cognitive flexibility.

Other results show that playing an instrument can increase your IQ by as many as seven points.

2. Our time management and organizational skills become improved.

Music, by nature, is timed. So in order to learn to play, students must learn to organize their thoughts in terms of time structures.

For instance, when learning a new piece, a student will begin to dissect the composition, focusing on the difficult passages first. This strategy is extremely efficient, and allows the student to progress more quickly as a musician.

When the student sees the resulting improvement, it creates even more motivation!

Therefore, music students will gradually train their brains to process *all* new information in terms of time and structure. This aids in the management and organization of tasks, extending far beyond the playing of their instruments.

3. Our coordination becomes enhanced

The sections of your brain that control motor skills actually grow larger and become more active when you learn to play a musical instrument.

In order to create music that sounds like music, your brain must translate thoughts and notations into specific motor patterns. As a result, your brain learns to master fingerings, rhythm, and even breathing, all at once!

Plus, for most instruments, you need to be able to have your fingers, arms, and sometimes even your legs each performing different tasks at the same time. This enhanced coordination can aid students in sports, typing, dancing, and much more!

4. Music relieves stress

Playing music, or even just listening to it, is a great way to relieve stress.

It doesn't matter if the music is soothing or extremely exciting. Either will help you get lost in the sea of sound. And when you are totally immersed, it's much easier to relax!

Playing an instrument also releases endorphins into your body, which naturally reduces your stress level.

5. Our memory capacity and empathy increases.

Playing a musical instrument helps the mind to be alert and remain active, eventually improving the memory.

Learning a foreign language, for instance, will become easier. Musicians also tend to be more accurate in interpreting other people's emotions.

Playing an instrument requires you to recognize sounds and tones. This increases your ability to store audio information, allowing for more proficiency in your own language, too.

6. Our aptitude for math skyrockets

Playing music requires the counting of notes and rhythms. This helps to reinforce and improve math skills.

The concepts and ideas involved with music theory are heavily influenced by mathematical concepts.

Students of music have a much easier time understanding concepts about fractions, percentages, and even geometry, because they already have experience with similar thought patterns.

7. Our confidence and self-expression become ignited!

When you reach a certain point in your musical education, you'll be able to express yourself by playing whatever kind of music you want.

You might even write your own music, and it could be in a whole new style that no one has even heard yet!

Music can become a great outlet for your emotions.

Playing a musical instrument builds self-esteem and a strong sense of identity.

8. Playing music provides health benefits.

Playing music has many soothing effects on the mind and body.

Studies suggest that music therapy helps children and teens with attention deficit hyperactivity disorder (ADHD), insomnia, and depression. Playing music has been found to reduce blood pressure levels in musicians of all ages.

Also, drumming, or rocking out some wild moves on another instrument, can burn as many as 500 calories during one session.

9. Music lessons teach discipline, responsibility and perseverance

It takes effort to learn how to play a musical instrument. And when you start getting good at your new skill, you get to see just how much that effort has paid off.

It's ultimately up to the student to put in the work. Once you get to a certain level, you will realize that with dedication, the sky is the limit!

Maintaining a consistent practice schedule is important, as it trains the student to be disciplined. The lessons and skills learned from consistent practice builds commitment, and aids in many other aspects of life.

10. It's just plain fun!!!

Playing music is a blast!

There's nothing better than getting totally engrossed in the song blasting through your headphones, or raucously rocking out with friends or bandmates.

Even when you're just getting started, playing some basic songs is super fun! No matter how simple, there's nothing better than being able to say "I just made music!"

Chapter 2

Choosing an instrument

If you or your child have not yet chosen an instrument to play, I have a few pieces of advice for you to consider.

First off, desire is important! It should be an instrument you love hearing and really **want** to play.

But don't feel pressured. It's okay if you change your mind later. Some students start with an instrument and eventually switch to a different one. Just as students change & grow, so do their tastes and interests. The great thing is that a lot of what you learn on one instrument is directly transferrable to other instruments.

Let's take a look at a few things to consider with five of the most popular instruments.

Voice:

In a way, you're already set to go for vocal lessons. After all, you don't need to go out and buy a voice!

You'll want to pick up some books on vocal instruction. Your teacher, after having a lesson or two to get acquainted with your tastes, can recommend what will work best for you.

Also, you'll want to find backing tracks of the songs you'd like to sing. These are readily available on sites like YouTube.

Even though you don't have to hit keys or pluck strings when you sing, the voice is still a specific instrument, albeit one that is internal. Warm-ups and breathing techniques are fundamental to properly using your voice. Visualization and acting techniques will help you to learn how to express yourself when singing.

I also recommend that singers learn to play guitar or piano. This way, they can provide their own accompaniment. Plus, it will help you gain even more knowledge about music in general. Even just learning the basics will significantly increase the range of what you can do with your voice and your music.

Piano:

Many people are concerned that they will need a piano at home in order to take piano lessons. This is not the case! It is perfectly fine to start out on an inexpensive keyboard. For the first few years of learning, you will be familiarizing yourself with the notes up and down the keyboard. Generally speaking, the order and sounds of the keys remains the same, regardless of the brand or cost.

Some keyboards have weighted keys and feel very much like playing a real piano.

Other keyboards don't have weighted keys, and that's fine too. Actually, most of the piano sounds you hear in popular music are made on keyboards without weighted keys. The only difference is how it feels when pushing down.

Also, there are some keyboards made with smaller keys. These can work well for a young student just starting out.

Guitar:

When starting lessons, the most important thing is to pick the right guitar. If you don't have the right kind of guitar, pressing the strings down can be hard and painful.

There are electric guitars and acoustic guitars. Acoustic guitars are either steel string or nylon string.

Beginners should start on an electric or a nylon string acoustic guitar. Even then, I'd recommend speaking to an expert about what models of guitar are easier to finger. Getting an informed opinion is always a plus.

There are many high-quality, easy to finger guitars that are very affordable. It just takes a little time to find the right ones- an effort that will certainly pay off once you start to play.

Still, even with an easy to finger guitar, there is a period during the first few weeks where your fingertips will get a little sore. This is normal! Don't feel discouraged.

Your fingers will toughen up shortly, and pressing the strings will begin to feel as natural to you as any daily activity.

Violin:

First off, it's extremely important to have a violin that's the right size for you. If you are an adult, a full size (4/4) violin will be a good fit. For the younger student, a smaller instrument will most likely be more appropriate.

The best way to ensure that you have the proper size is to visit a store that specializes in stringed instruments. The professionals there will be able to measure you, and determine the size of violin that will best fit your body.

Beware of cheap violins in mail-order catalogues, online, or in stores that do not specialize in stringed instruments. Some of these are practically toys, and can be pretty much unplayable!

New violinists will learn to coordinate the fingering and the bowing of their instrument. And the lack of frets on the violin creates an additional challenge. As a result, a beginner violinist doesn't generally produce the most pleasant tones right away. So don't be dismayed if you or the student in your home sounds a bit squawky at first. This is all part of the process, and the tone will improve greatly over time.

Drums:

There are a few things to consider about starting drum lessons.

Most students want to start off playing the kit. If that's where the desire is, that's the direction to take. Do what makes the student happy!

However, it is also fine, and very common, to start off with some sticks and a practice pad. This is an inexpensive way to start learning some basic rhythms. If you choose to go this direction, I would recommend getting a kit within 3 to 4 months after starting. It's just a whole lot more exciting, and will keep the student's interest strong!

By nature, drums are loud! To preserve the ears, I recommend using shooter muffs or earplugs when playing for a long period of time. You can also practice by running a backing track through headphones!

Electronic drums are also an option. Depending on your living situation (and your desire to preserve a relationship with your neighbors!) it's nice to be able to turn the volume up or down.

Chapter 3

10 Things to look for in a music lessons provider

Not all music lessons are the same. It's important to find a lessons provider that will fulfill your needs as an individual. Here are some guidelines that I recommend:

1. Take lessons with a teacher who is fun. Having a teacher who has a fun, positive attitude makes learning easier. You will feel inspired and encouraged, like you can take on the world!

2. Take lessons at a school designed for private lessons. In-home lessons or lessons at a teacher's house are riddled with distractions. Phone calls, texting, household tasks, cooking smells, and other disruptions can lead to non-productive lesson time. Plus, many students end up feeling *too* comfortable at home, which can lead to a more lax attitude during lessons.

Often, teachers involved in these kinds of lessons lack structure in their lesson plans.

A school designed for private lessons should have an office staff who takes care of all the scheduling, so the teacher is free to focus all of their attention on you. When teachers are distracted by things like scheduling and client phone calls, it can be difficult for them to focus on their priorities. A teacher's #1 priority should always be to give you the best lesson experience possible.

3. Take lessons at a school run by a music lessons authority. There are many factors involved with teaching private music lessons. When a school is run by not just a businessperson or musician, but someone who has many years of teaching experience, they know specifically what to look for in teachers they hire at their school.

4. Take lessons at a school that has multiple teachers for each instrument. Music teachers come and go. Like all of us, they sometimes have to move or experience unavoidable family commitments. I had several guitar teachers when I was young. When you take lessons at a school with multiple teachers, changing teachers becomes easy. These teachers were all hired by the same music lessons authority and thus have similar teaching styles. If your teacher leaves or stops teaching when you aren't taking lessons at a school like this, you have to start the whole process over to find another good teacher.

5. Take lessons with a teacher who will teach you the music you want to play. This seems like a given, but actually, many teachers insist on teaching in the same style in which they were taught. These teachers don't pay attention to what their students are interested in, because they are hung-up on one particular teaching method. You will want to start with a teacher who is extremely versatile and can show you how to play not only by the book, but also by ear. The best teachers also utilize available technology, like laptops and tablets.

6. Take lessons at a place with a pleasant atmosphere and a community of like-minded students. When you see others around you taking lessons and having fun, it inspires you to stick with it and become truly amazing!

7. Take lessons from a provider who offers at least two recitals a year. Every student deserves the opportunity to perform in recitals. After all, they are your chance to show off all that talent and hard work!

Many students feel nervous before their first recital. Nervousness is normal, and can even be seen as a positive—it shows that you care about what you are doing! The truth is, you will gain so much confidence after having performed. Recitals can really help students move forward, as they are a great way to set concrete goals. Also, it's fun and inspiring to see what the other students do!

Despite the benefits, recitals should never be mandatory. Students should choose to participate when they are ready. Sometimes it builds confidence to just come and watch.

8. Take lessons at a school that hosts community events throughout the year. Events like these are important, because they help a student build relationships. Often, you will get the chance to hear your teacher perform, and you are likely to meet fellow students who have similar interests to yours. When you become an active part of something larger, you no longer feel like you're doing it on your own. You will have a new support system. Getting more involved creates enthusiasm, because it's simply much more exciting!

9. Take lessons at a place clients rave about. Does your lessons provider have testimonials on their website? And what do they say? When you find a place where the clients' words really resonate with you, that's where you should go.

10. Did I mention that you should take lessons from somewhere that's fun? I know I did, but I want to stress it one more time! Students who enjoy their lessons do so much better and progress so much faster.

Lessons should have structure. Lessons should be informative. Lessons should be inspiring. And...

Music lessons should be fun!

Benefits of taking music lessons for people of different ages

Lessons aren't just for one age group! Next, I will address some benefits that students of different ages will be privy to by taking music lessons. Again, these are by no means the only benefits, just some of the most noteworthy.

Chapter 4

Benefits of music lessons for children

1. Children who take music lessons often have larger vocabularies and better reading skills than children who do not take lessons.

2. Children who take music lessons are more likely to excel in various forms of study, work more effectively in teams, exhibit better critical thinking skills, stay enrolled in school, graduate, and pursue higher education.

3. Recent studies have shown that children who start and continue with music lessons statistically have lower reports of substance abuse (tobacco, alcohol, and illicit drugs.)

4. Children who play music typically spend less time watching TV.

5. Children who play music display higher self-esteem and are more optimistic.

Chapter 7

Benefits of music lessons for the whole family

Quite often, when a child or teen student begins taking music lessons, a sibling or parent will start taking lessons as well. Although such family support is not necessary to become a wonderful musician on your own, it's still a great idea! Here are some of the benefits.

1. It's easier to maintain a practice schedule when there's more than one person participating. It's practice time, and the whole family knows it!

2. Healthy competition can push multiple family members to strive for their best.

3. Family members with advanced abilities can help the others out. Teaching family members can be a great way to practice!

4. It can be fun to play together as a family.

5. Mini-recitals in your living room! These can be used to push students to reach small goals.

Chapter 8

10 Practicing tips

1. Practice every day

It's very important to maintain a consistent practicing routine. Everyone has unavoidable conflicts, so it's okay to skip a day or two here and there. But if this happens, try to catch up with two practice sessions the day after.

When you practice with your instrument daily, it becomes a larger and more integral part of your life.

Consistency helps you retain what you have learned, and it helps you to see your progress.

Research has found that when you do something all the time, you will even dream about it when you sleep. That means your brain will actually continue to improve your abilities while you're sleeping!

2. **When starting, practice for about 10 to 15 minutes each day.**

Do not over-practice and turn it into a chore.

Keep your practice sessions light and simple.

This will help you retain a more positive attitude about practicing.

The key is to do this every day, and make it a part of your regular routine. We don't think twice about brushing our teeth every night, and it can be the same for practicing!

After a while, you will become ready to practice more, because you will really **want** to practice more.

3. Leave your instrument out where you can see it.

If you have an instrument that goes in a case, take it out of the case once you get home from your lesson.

Put it in a prominent, noticeable place.

Having it in plain sight will remind you to practice each day.

This will also show you that music is a part of your life, and that you are becoming a real musician!

Plus, if you have friends over, they will probably think it's pretty cool that you have an instrument. And guess what? IT IS COOL!

Singers should leave out books and CDs with backing tracks.

4. **Put posters or pictures of your favorite musicians up in your practice area.**

It doesn't matter if you practice in your bedroom, basement, or another area of your house or apartment. You should consider decorating at least part of it, to make it feel more like your designated practicing area.

When you do this, similar to leaving your instrument out, you reinforce the fact that you are a musician. It can really shift your mindset!

You can also find clocks, lamps, and many other items that are shaped like your instrument.

Any kind of music-related imagery can work. You can even clip photos from old books and magazines. It's all about making it personal!

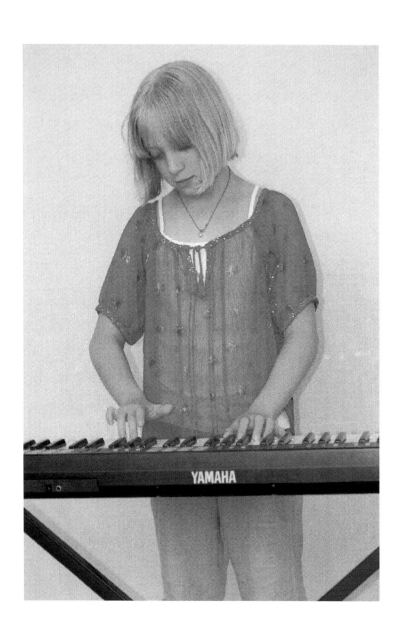

5. **Practice at the same time each day.**

Find a time that you will consistently have free for *Practice Time.*

Then, stick with that time every day.

This way, it becomes a natural part of your daily routine.

When practicing is ingrained into your regular schedule, it is hard to forget to do it!

Also, visualization is helpful. When you think about that time of the day, form a picture of it in your mind, and get excited about it! Imagine your practice session as a big step toward becoming the musician of your dreams.

6. Your attitude will take you far!

When you are learning to play a musical instrument, some things will be fun right away and some things will be more difficult.

Keep in mind that it might take more time to master certain lessons.

Never assume that something being hard means you're doing badly.

Always remember that with some more practice, you will get it down.

If you put in the effort, nothing will stop you. You will be AWESOME!

Keep that attitude with you always.

7. **Parents need to tell their kids to practice.**

Often, kids will not practice on their own.
Actually, that's an understatement. Children will
almost never practice without serious prompting.

Some of my advice here will help, but it's
ultimately up to parents to get their kids to
practice.

It's a great idea to make a weekly or monthly
chart. Then, you can place little stickers on each
day your children practice. Getting the chart
filled with stickers is a great incentive.

Or take it one step further--once they attain a
certain number of stickers, you can treat them to
ice cream, a movie, museum, or whatever your
kids love.

Once they've been practicing for a while, it will
become habit, and your kids will start taking

initiative on their own. Eventually they will thank you for pushing them!

8. Practice slowly to master quickly.

When they are first starting out, most students want to rush. It's great to be eager, but in this case, slow and steady definitely wins.

It's always important to practice very slowly when you are starting something new.

When practicing, do it as slowly as you need to be able to play it accurately. Even if it is really, really slow.

If you go too fast for yourself, you will repeatedly make mistakes. Then, your subconscious starts to believe that you can't do it.

When you slow it down enough to succeed, your brain says, "Hey, I can do this!"

Once you perfect it at a slow pace, gradually work on getting faster. You will!

9. **Watch other musicians and pretend you are them when you practice.**

It's always helpful to look at someone who really knows how to play.

You can find clips on the internet, watch TV, a DVD, or see someone play live.

Observe what they are doing and how they look while they are playing.

Then, when you are playing a song or practicing, pretend you are that musician!

This technique, called modeling, can be very effective for learning and building confidence.

You can also use your teacher as someone to model.

10. **Set goals for what you want to learn and when you want to learn it by.**

Having specific goals and deadlines will help increase your motivation levels.

When you are a new student, your teacher can help evaluate what goals will be attainable for you.

Later on, you will have the experience to judge for yourself what you can accomplish within a specific time period.

Think of it like a game. A fun challenge!

And if you picture it in these terms, you will want to WIN! What a great incentive!

Chapter 9

A new way of taking lessons

We live in a world that is constantly changing and reinventing itself. Through technology and human ingenuity, we find new ways of doing things almost daily.

One of the new possibilities for students of music is taking online lessons.

Taking live, online lessons with an instructor at a professional music school is a close second to actually being there.

Again, to be clear, the lessons **must** come from a real brick and mortar school. Here, there is no doubt about the quality of your instructors. Your teachers will have been hired by a trusted, highly-experienced music lessons authority, who has put them through the necessary background checks. There should also be an office staff that handles all the scheduling.

The bottom line is that everything should be run and handled just like the music school I mentioned in Chapter 3. *DO NOT SETTLE FOR PRE-RECORDED VIDEOS OR A RANDOM TEACHER SITTING IN A LIVING ROOM.*

There are many online lessons available that offer pre-recorded videos. These can get you started, but they are not tailored to you as an individual. You may end up learning from a specific method which isn't right for you. Plus, you can't ask questions or get advice specific to what you are practicing. Usually, the lack of communication involved with this method leads to frustration and alienation from the instrument.

There are also many websites that will connect you with teachers who have listed themselves as being available. Unfortunately, in these situations, there is no real screening process. It's difficult to tell if any of these teachers are right for you. They were never interviewed by someone with experience in what to look for in a teacher. Most often, they are teaching out of their living rooms without immediate access to the necessary tools for teaching.

When online lessons are done right, you get to virtually attend a professionally-run music school, where the teachers have been hand-picked by a music lessons authority. The teacher will not be distracted during the lessons. Plus, you and your teacher can communicate and tailor the lessons to your interests and skill level, getting you on the path to playing the music you love.

I highly recommend trying this type of online lessons if there isn't a suitable music school near you.

Chapter 10

Finding your place in music

It's probably pretty obvious that I'm passionate about music and about private music lessons. Running a music school and writing a book are huge commitments.

I believe, based on both personal experience and what I've learned from others, that music lessons have something very special to offer a student.

It doesn't matter if you're doing it as a hobby, or if you have aspirations of becoming a professional musician. The benefits are numerous.

It has been a true pleasure and honor to have worked with thousands of students over my career. In teaching these students, I have learned so much.

I have learned how music can bring us all together. How it is universal, and can touch the hearts of people from all walks of life.

I have learned that we are all individuals. That there are as many different ways to learn as there are people. There is no right or wrong way to learn. Talented teachers can work with students to find the methods that work best for each.

I have learned that music plants the seeds of optimism, and can help nurture happiness.

But my favorite thing is the opportunity I've had to learn a bit about each student's life. I've gotten to see how music has affected them in so many positive ways!

If you or a family member are thinking about starting music lessons, I highly encourage you to do so.

It has been the best thing I've ever gotten involved with, and I know you'll love it, too!

All of the principles and philosophies outlined in this book have been applied to my physical music academy in Rochester New York,

Rochester Academy of Music & Arts
RochesterMusicLessons.com

and my online academy at
VirtualAcademyofMusic.com

95

Whether you are near or far, you or someone you love can benefit from taking lessons at one of my music academies.

If you live in the Rochester New York area, visit Rochester Academy of Music & Arts at:

RochesterMusicLessons.com

If you live outside of the Rochester New York area or have trouble getting to our physical location, visit us at:

VirtualAcademyofMusic.com

You may also call (585) 506-9437 to talk about either academy with our friendly and helpful office staff.